D1241611

The Posters of Picasso

POSTERS

OF

PICASSO

CALVIN T. RYAN LIBRARY
U. OF NEBRASKA AT KEARNEY

EDITED AND WITH AN INTRODUCTION BY

JOSEPH K. FOSTER

CROWN PUBLISHERS, INC., NEW YORK

ACKNOWLEDGMENTS

The editor and publisher gratefully acknowledge the generous co-operation of the following:

The Museum of Modern Art, New York, for the use of posters reproduced on Plates 1, 2, & 5.

Mrs. Daniel B. Fuller, New York, for the use of the poster reproduced on Plate 14.

Mr. Henry Kahnweiler, Paris, for the poster reproduced on Plate 12.

Mr. Gene Fenn, Paris, for the poster reproduced on Plate 22.

© 1957, BY CROWN PUBLISHERS, INC.

LIBRARY OF CONGRESS CATALOG CARD NUMBER: 57-12822

PRINTED IN THE UNITED STATES BY YORK LITHO CO.,

ANDY PERNI, TECHNICAL SUPERVISOR.

For Lydia

THIS is the era of the psyche, no less than it is that of the atom. For the psychic involvements of the emotions you go to the analysts, for the problems of communications you go to the sales experts. In the command posts of advertising they say that the poster has more or less outlived its commercial usefulness. While it is still effective in certain areas, "the psychology of communication" requires more up-to-date techniques of mass beguilement.

It is generally true, of course, that national (as well as local) newspaper advertising, radio, television, and even sky-writing, has in the last seventy-five years replaced the poster as a means of reaching the multitudes. But as a method of direct appeal, the poster has yet to meet its master. The cost of spreading a message nationally by this method is prohibitive, obviously, and only agencies as puissant and as rich as governments or the Red Cross can afford it. Yet in national emergencies such as wars, the poster plays as powerful a role as it did in the days when there was no radio or television. In places where posters are collected, one can come upon the powerful World War I posters exhibiting the blood-curdling barbarities of the Hun. Of the same period was the striking American recruiting poster with a picture of Uncle Sam pointing a compelling finger at every passerby under a caption which declaimed "Uncle Sam Wants You." So powerful was this poster that even women (this was before the advent of the WAC, etc.) and children felt they were being personally singled out.

Both sides of the American Civil War used posters in great quantity. During the Spanish Civil War the government relied almost exclusively on posters as a means of reaching its supporters, particularly after some of its other channels of communication had broken down. It is also generally acknowledged that the maker of the poster must subscribe, in great measure, to the message of his creation if it is to be effective. Otherwise, despite all the advantages of the medium, the design will lack conviction and, hence, results. Thus the poster makes great demands upon the makers thereof for the same reason that it influences the onlooker. The poster-maker is dealing with direct speech, so to speak.

In one sense, the poster, far from losing its place in the field of mass visual persuasion, has extended its sway incalculably. At the turn of the century, most newspaper advertising appeared in the form of what we today call "classified" advertising — three- or four-line paragraphs of agate type listed in single-column width down the page without embellishments or illustration. The popularity of the poster and its effect on advertisers altered the newspaper and magazine ad in design and appearance to what is known today as the "display ad." This form of advertisement uses color, special layout, and lettering and in general utilizes all the principles of poster advertising.

The poster itself has, of course, changed in stature to a noticeable extent through the years. In the early days of the poster, when it was used as a public announcement, there was little thought given to its form or design or the problems of composition. It was, in a manner of speaking, unaware of itself as an art form. But it is no longer so innocent. Since the days of Cheret the poster has become a self-conscious art. Artists such as Delacroix, Daumier and Gavarni before him, had used the poster, but it did not assume its present position of respect until the last decade of the nineteenth century after Toulouse-Lautrec, imparting to it the characteristics of his general art, demonstrated its widespread effectiveness in new fields. Since then, other artists began to use the poster form with increasing frequency, and business firms turned to the established painters with commissions for work. Bonnard, Fantin-Latour, Matisse, Braque, as well as Picasso, appeared regularly in this medium. Books on the art of the poster and on various poster collections and on the poster work of different countries began to appear. International Poster Annuals became a regular feature of the fine art and advertising worlds. The poster developed its own critical language and criteria. Poster exhibits were soon accepted by the art-conscious public as a regular feature of the cultural landscape.

Although the poster may have lost its original place as a commercial advertising medium, as a form of graphic art it had come to stay.

The growth of the poster as a graphic art has been further stimulated by the publishers of art prints and reproductions. The better samples of poster art, those most original in design and color as well as those bearing the signature of "name" artists, are manufactured by the thousands and sold all over the country as appendages of interior decoration. The home bar, the "rumpus room," the game room, the converted or finished cellar in the homes of the new suburban communities have all created a demand for gay, inexpensive types of wall decoration—a demand appropriately supplied by the contemporary poster.

Since the war, interest in the collecting of poster originals has grown steadily. Many people who cannot afford expensive oil paintings are eager to own original etchings and lithographs. Originally designed posters fell into the category of and are still regarded as original lithographs. The collecting of posters by prominent artists was begun before the war but really reached a sweeping momentum after the war. The originally-pulled posters of Lautrec and Bonnard were in constant demand both by individuals and museums. Today it is common practice — particularly in France, where the original posters of Matisse, Braque, Chagall, Miró, and Picasso are published — for art dealers to buy a batch of each fresh edition of posters designed by these artists, hold them a while, and then sell them at bloated prices to art collectors, art students, tourists seeking gifts, etc. It is not uncommon, for instance, to see a Picasso poster that was originally published in connection with a ceramic exhibit or a bullfight and sold for about two dollars, offered six months or a year later, when the original edition has been exhausted, at an art gallery for anywhere from $75 to $250.

Very often posters are printed in limited editions on better paper for the fancier trade. Many posters are also published twice, once with the lettering announcing the event for which the poster was designed and once again without the lettering to give the collectors an additional prize to go after. Often a limited edition will be signed and numbered by the artist and sold as a hard-to-get lithograph, divorced from its commercial affiliation. In fact, so popular is an original poster by a major artist that the art dealer planning an exhibit by such an artist will count on the sale of the poster advertising the show to defray his expenses.

Permanent exhibits of posters exist in several places in Paris. Michel's on the Quai Saint-Michel

has one of Lautrec while the Maison de la Pensée Française has one of Picasso and the Galerie Maeght maintains permanent poster shows of Braque and Chagall. Lautrec posters flooded the United States — in reproduction of course — in connection with the film *Moulin Rouge* and have been selling steadily ever since. The featuring of these posters in the film itself had much to do with

FIGURE 1

the subsequent popularity of these works.

We find, then, two dominant impulses in the collecting of these posters: the desire to own the poster as a lithograph original, and to put up as colorful decoration the popularized poster of a well-known artist, whether it be an original or a reproduction. This second custom has been responsible for the popularity of lesser or unknown artists who produce work that is decorative and gay. Thus the small poster, usually about 24 x 32 inches, has flourished mightily.

Any discussion of Picasso as a poster artist would be incomplete without first summarizing the main forces and influences that brought French poster art to its present eminence in the field. Despite contrary claims, it is generally agreed that France was the birthplace of the poster as a graphic art, and it was there that the poster, as we know it today, was developed and brought to full fruition. Gavarni, the printmaker, produced a poster as early as 1847 and was followed by Delacroix shortly after. Daumier made the first illustrated

FIGURE 2

commercial poster, a commission from a coal warehouse. The French industrialists, it must be admitted, were first-rate opportunists who realized the value of having established artists design their commercial posters. But France also produced a brilliant line of graphic artists, whose reputation was made almost exclusively in the poster field and from whom the fine artists learned a great

deal. The center of this group was the Chaix Studios in Paris, and it began to make itself felt about 1880. During the preceding half-century or so the stone had replaced the wood block for most commercial printing purposes. Printing from the stone permitted a more fluid use of color, as a result of which printing in color increased considerably. This first stone-process in color printing was known as chromolithography. The use of color in poster work had existed before, but it had been put in chiefly by hand. Although we have many beautiful examples of color work created by chromolithography, the poor taste of the merchants who ordered printing was reflected in both design and execution of the work done. The epoch of chromolithography was soon stigmatized as a period of low taste and gave rise to the word "chromo," a disdainful condemnation of any color work lacking in quality or distinction.

The artists of the Chaix Studio happily rescued the poster from this sterile condition. Working at this studio were several artists including Steinlen *(Figure 1)* Ibels, Willette, Grosset, and Cheret who brought original design, imagination, and spirit to their work. The most skillful artist of this group, the most prolific and ultimately the best known was Jules Cheret. He became recognized, through his inventions and innovations, as the father of the modern color poster. Yet, although he successfully separated or helped separate the poster from the curse of chromoism, his work is full of many of the characteristics of Victorian decoration, or rather its French parallel — an elaboration of detail, a lack of subtlety, profusion rather than economy of line and detail, etc. — aspects of the art that Lautrec, a contemporary, later eliminated. Yet Cheret had a bravura and dash to his themes (see *Figures 2 and 3*) that made his posters highly decorative. His color, too, was bold and full, a vast improvement on the muddy tones and tints of the preceding decades. He created the technique, later vastly improved by Lautrec, of shading the background and softening the area around the central characters to bring them into sharp focus. Cheret became a vogue, and other artists began to collect him. The habit of collecting had not yet reached the people, or even the professional collector, but this movement by the artists of France had its effect. Other artists began to copy his pictorial style and soon a whole school of poster design was flourishing. The poster, as a result, was used in increasingly larger quantities, and began to attract the attention of the fine-artists in growing numbers.

At this point a minimum of technical explanation may be pertinent, since lithography is the process that most contemporary artists use in the creation of posters.

In lithographic printing, the artist draws upon the stone with a grease pencil or greasy paint. Grease repels water, but the ungreased surface of the stone holds it. When greasy ink is applied, it is rejected by the wet parts of the stone and retained by the parts marked out by the artist. In short, the ink is held where the artist puts down his greasy area. The paper is then applied to the inked areas and the image is transferred to the paper. This is done for each color and for as many colors as are desired.

The advantage of this method over the stiff techniques such as the wood block is obvious. It permits full color, full-scale drawings done in continuous line, thus enabling the poster artist to turn out pictures comparable to paintings.

In the United States at the turn of the century, offset lithography replaced stone lithography. That is, lithography was now done by automatic machine instead of by hand. In this process, metal is used instead of stone since metal can be made to bend around the cylinder of a printing press. In addition to the direct methods of placing the image on the surface, whether stone or metal, it is also possible to transfer the image from paper, canvas or any other surface onto the metal plate by means of photography. A later advance was the addition to the press of a rubber roller or blanket. The metal plate sets off its image onto the rubber roller, which transfers the image to the paper. This technique is used in most cases of lithographic printing and is sometimes referred to as photolithography. The general name, however, is offset lithography. This is the process by which this book was printed.

This is essentially the method that Picasso employs in the production of his posters; the stone is rarely used and then only to practice an almost forgotten virtuosity, or where mechanical offset presses are not available.

The introduction of offset lithography opened the gates to mass printing and distribution, and it soon became possible to publish one poster in an edition of scores of thousands.

In the last half-century the changes in the art of poster printing have been refinements rather than any alteration of basic principles. To begin with,

FIGURE 3

the metal plates are now produced with grainless surfaces. The printing inks are vastly different from the inks of the Ault & Wiborg Co., for whom Toulouse-Lautrec designed a poster. They are clearer and truer in the intensity of the hues. Photographic films from which the image is transferred to the metal plate contain more sensitized emulsion and thus produce a truer image with regard to sharpness and color.

The screen used in this process has been refined to the point where it is possible to get a clean image without clogging, even when using a screen that registers 200 dots to the inch. The advantage of this improvement can be more easily grasped when one considers that the photographs used in magazines, for instance, contain no more than 90 to 120 dots to the inch. The screen is visible in such instances, and even more so in newspapers which use an even coarser screen. In short, so fine a screen produces so clean a surface that the screen is not detectable except under a magnifying glass. Papers too have improved with regard to surface, tensile strength, opacity, and so on. Lenses without aberration or distortion are now commonplace in camera work. All these improvements make for finer printing, producing better artistic results and losing less and less of the artist's original work in the process of reproduction.

Although it is true that Jules Cheret is regarded as the father of the modern color poster, it is equally true that up to the contemporary era, dominated by Picasso, no man influenced the direction of the modern poster as much as Toulouse-Lautrec. As a contemporary of the Chaix Studio group, he was undoubtedly influenced by Cheret and others. But such influence did not last long. Like Gauguin and Van Gogh, he was much more impressed and affected by the techniques of the Japanese printmakers, whose works were introduced into Europe in the late nineteenth century *(Figure 4)*. Like those of Bonnard, his posters exhibit the same flat areas, the same simplicity

of design. His colors, although subtle and often used with great cunning and brilliance, were used as the Japanese used color, to emphasize composition and construction. He also took the most conventional subjects, emphasizing the most commonplace ideas, such as girls singing, couples dancing, etc., and in an unencumbered and highly original manner infused them with drama and importance. Midinettes turned dance-hall entertainers became stars of international magnitude as a result of his memorable posters. He introduced Jane Avril, May Milton, May Belfort, Aristide Bruant, Mlle. Eglantine to his contemporaries and to posterity. If we did not have his posters, they would be remembered, if at all, merely as a small footnote to the history of nineteenth-century Parisian culture.

In the area of design he went considerably beyond the school of Cheret. Whereas this group merely dimmed the figures and details surround-

FIGURE 4

ing the central characters in order to emphasize their importance, Lautrec eliminated entirely details that were not connected with his main figures, and indicated everything else with only a blob of color, or a series of identifying lines. In his famous "Divan Japonais," Avril and her English toff are seated at a bar that is given substance only by her bag, while an orchestra is indicated by some outlines of instruments and the leader's baton. All elements are fused into a general background with an economy of detail that was brand new in the poster field. In his "Moulin Rouge," the atmosphere of revelry and abandon around La Goulue and the rail-thin Valentin is created by a circle of yellow dabs indicating brilliant lighting. The silhouetting of a circle of top hats indicate that the gay blades and men-about-town are out in full strength. This economy of line and elimination of unnecessary detail had a great influence on the poster designers who followed, both among fine and commercial artists, and shaped Picasso's early work considerably.

Lautrec took his poster work with great seriousness. He began every poster project with a series of preliminary studies in oil. When he was satisfied with the final result, he took the painting to the lithographers and worked from it, often for days on end, until he was satisfied with the results.

Lautrec also gained dramatic effects in his posters through the exaggeration of figures and gestures. One need only recall the posters featuring Aristide Bruant, Yvette Guilbert, May Milton, Jane Avril in the Jardin de Paris and numerous others. He cut loose from the traditional habits of his predecessors, but even more he used his tools with a boldness that gave a new dimension to stone printing. In all, he completed thirty-one posters that constituted a legacy for the future of poster art.

The world of business was quick to realize the potent effect on the cash till of the well-executed poster, and before long commissions of all sorts were pouring in on Lautrec and his contemporaries. Publishing houses, camera-supply houses, night clubs and music halls, theatres, even a printing ink company in the United States employed the graphic talents of the artists. Lautrec also designed some two dozen song-sheets that served as the first pages of sheet music scores (see *Figures 5* and *6*). These were in effect small posters, and proved so effective that the practice spread around the world. It became a commonplace in the cities of Paris, London, New York, etc., to see the front pages of sheet music arranged in elaborate display in the windows of the music stores, creating attractive splashes of color where only staid rows of dull notes or elaborately engraved paper existed before. It is no exaggeration to say that these colorful displays stimulated business wherever they were used consistently.

In the midst of the increasing use of the poster by men of artistic reputation and talent, one curi-

FIGURE 5

12

ous fact stands out. The poster was avoided as a means of publicizing the art show. In the late nineteenth and early twentieth century, a single small sign outside the exhibition hall sufficed. It was felt that although the poster was good enough for business, it would not do to confuse the patrons by admitting that fine and graphic art shared the same lofty niche. This was more the thinking of the exhibitor than of the artist. This reticence did not disappear until after World War I. Today in Europe an exhibit is seldom arranged without including a poster by the artist of the works exhibited as part of the show. This is far from true in this country, where gallery owners seldom advertise an art exhibit by means of a poster. In France, which fathered the tradition, the practice flourishes more strongly than ever. Café bulletin-boards are covered to overflowing with poster announcements of various art activities; store windows all display the posters; and when large retrospective exhibits of well-known artists are arranged poster announcements decorate the lamp posts on all the main boulevards. Lobbies of hotels, large or small, run-down or de luxe, display art posters along with information on the theatre and the ballet. Such artists as Picasso, Miró, Braque, Chagall, Léger, Dufy, Matisse, and Derain are among the hundreds of artists who have produced posters in connection with exhibits of their work.

Despite the numerous reasons for the increased interest in poster usage — the advance in technical methods; the influence of such men as Cheret, Bonnard, Lautrec, and Steinlen; and the increasing number of men engaged in the creation of posters (over two hundred men in Paris alone by 1900) — the art declined after World War I. If the war was a climax in the use of posters, then the immediate postwar period was an anticlimax. Not only did their social use drop off sharply, but the quality of the posters became exceedingly poor. In France the years 1919 to 1925 marked a low stage

FIGURE 6

in this branch of graphic expression. Posters of this period were exceedingly dull and unimaginative. The war had erased old methods and styles, the techniques of former years were now inadequate to express the moods and feelings and needs of the depressed postwar world. Furthermore, the depression or recession that follows every war spread a blanket of conservatism on both taste and spending among businessmen the world over.

This condition persisted until about 1925 when the brilliant Cassandre and Paul Colin appeared in Paris like a breath of fresh air to set new powerful standards in graphic design, standards and styles that persist more or less to the present day.

Another factor that brought freshness and new feeling to poster design was the growth of montage or collage, with its attendant practice of *papier collé*, a technique that was based upon the combination of symbols to create a definite message.

The words come from the French and mean literally mountings or pasteups. In addition to the Dadaists, such artists as Schwitters, the Surrealists, and the Cubists, led by Picasso, Braque, Léger and Gris, one of the most important theoreticians of the art of montage was Serge Eisenstein, the famous Russian film director. He claimed that montage was based on the premise that one image combined with a second produced a conclusion or third image, which bore no relation to either of the first two separately but was the summation of the first two used together. For instance, you may show a Negro getting into a car with a couple of white men. This image in itself has no special meaning, especially if all the individuals behave quietly and with decorum. You may then show a separate image of the white men getting into a car with a coil of rope. That, too, in itself has no particular meaning. But the moment you combine both images, that is, a Negro getting into a car with some white men carrying a rope, the combined images produce a dramatic shock whose meaning is all too clear.

A famous poster showing the orderly rows of a cotton field as background to a rope looped and knotted, eloquently called attention to the ever-present threat of lynching. One of the most poignant antiwar posters ever published showed an abandoned baby sitting in a field of rubble. Or take the well-known anti-accident poster showing a boy's cap and a broken bicycle on a highway, or an equally well-known aperitif poster showing a table with two partially filled glasses, a pair of women's gloves, and a partially consumed cigarette still burning in an ashtray—all suggestively framed by folds of drapery. In all of these instances two symbols not necessarily related to each other were combined to produce a third meaning resulting from their combination.

The power of such combinations may sometimes lead to false presumptions. This truism is illustrated by the much-aired story of the young woman

in mourning clothes placing flowers at a grave and then contemplating the tombstone with quiet grief. A man approaches and tries to console the woman. "Madam," he says, "I know that it is difficult for you to realize that you will someday find another man, and that life will again be good and full." "Sir," the young woman replied, "this *is* the other man."

The use of montage imparted great flexibility and variety to the field of graphic art, and the result was a movement that produced a steady

FIGURE 7

stream of great posters.

The secret of Cassandre's success (see *Figure 7*) lay in his use of abstract design. He went back to the intellectual and aesthetic ideas that were developing in Europe in the decade immediately preceding World War I.

Picasso, of course, as a leader in the Cubist movement, dominated the art of the period, and

14

unquestionably had great effect on Cassandre's ideas and designs. Cassandre used type not only as an integral part of the design (an idea that was common to both Cheret and Toulouse-Lautrec) but very often designed the lettering to dominate the poster.

Cassandre contended that ". . . a poster is meant to be seen and noticed *by people who do not try to see it . . .*" Therefore, any method, short of bad taste and bad composition, is valid if it arrests the attention of the indifferent potential viewer. This viewer, it must be remembered, is confronted with a complex of unassorted impressions as he moves along, preoccupied with his own private thoughts and problems. With this thought in mind, Cassandre evolved a system of bold designs, with large striking bands of contrasting color to carry out these designs. The abstract technique that he depended on utilizes an economy of line with just enough detail to make the meaning clear. Cassandre felt that as a poster designer he was committed to the task of making his meaning clear while making his design as eye-catching and as striking as possible. This added up to an originally expressed idea in terms of common meaning. Less successful artists, in an attempt to capture originality of design, often became too abstract and hence obscured the meaning of the poster, thus rendering it useless for all practical purposes. The problem has been astutely summed up by Maximillien Vox, the French type designer. "Painting is a self-sufficient proposition; not so the poster — a means, a short cut . . . a kind of telegraph. The poster artist does not *issue* a message, he merely passes it on. No one asks for his opinion, he is only expected to establish a connection." This definition of the poster artist is applicable only to the commercial poster man working under certain conditions. The poster mounted on highway boards must be so designed as to meet the eye even more quickly than those posted in the city. He must design posters of what has come to be known as the

"DO-BUY-SEE-GO school," a form of attention-getting that later gave rise to the one-word magazines like *Look, See, Pic,* etc., and to the manufactured articles of similarly brief identification. All subtleties must be sacrificed to the central message expressed in a minimum number of words and boldly proclaimed.

The demands on the poster artist vary enorm-

FIGURE 8

ously and the designer of a poster meant to be used in the subway has much greater latitude than other of his colleagues. To a large extent, he is dealing with a captive audience which has a certain amount of leisure. Thus he can inject humor, comedy, drama, narrative. He can even be non-objective, provided the spectator has time to look at the poster for a few minutes.

In Paris, where the subway traveler has even greater leisure than he has here, the poster artists go in for subtlety and humor to a large extent.

Another factor that shapes poster design in Paris is the existence of the outdoor café or terrace. On the theory that the average Frenchman spends some part of the twenty-four hours on one of these terraces, the poster artist fashions his product for the man who enjoys leisure and relaxation while looking. Thus, the works of Savignac in his incomparable Perrier series, for instance, possess humor, ingenuity, subtlety, and all the pleasurable qualities of a clever magazine cartoon that is perused in one's own good time.

All the schools of poster artists, for all their differences, share one function in common: the objective of moving the spectator to action. The contemporary commercial poster artist, whatever his field of action, stresses a minimum use of line. Occasionally, when the requirement warrants it, the artist may do a full painting, but by and large he uses a shorthand method of communication.

His methods of design and use of color stem directly from the innovations of the fine artists. The origins of the work of such leading designers as Berard and Vertès, for instance, are indicated quite clearly. One need but look at the illustrations in this volume to see how the economy of line developed in the continuity of poster design. First Lautrec chipped away at the superfluity of detail that characterized the work of Cheret. Bonnard went a step further. His poster in the Salon de Cent series *(Figure 8)* is typical of his calligraphic invention. One bold line defines the lady's costume, and the line representing the dog's leash completes the total construction of his theme. Thus with a couple of bold strokes he has created the full atmosphere suggested by the subject. Matisse *(Figure 9)* puts down bold, flat areas of black and yellow on a white ground to create depth and drama in an overpowering composition. The whole work glows and pulsates with an inner intensity. He uses color in the manner of the Japanese printmakers, to construct his areas and to endow his work with solidity and force. Braque, another modern master *(Figure 10)* who often rests upon linear invention for his effects, here works out a quick and continuous line without even taking his crayon off the paper. He is a craftsman who also eliminates all but the barest essentials. Like Picasso, he creates the form but never imprisons it. A simple whitewash background indicates the endless sky and in turn the limitless soaring flight of the bird. The newspaper background behind it is partially a throwback to the days of the *papier collé*, in which a touch of everyday reality is injected into an exercise of imagination. It is also used in this instance to emphasize the casualness, the spur-of-the-moment feeling that he wishes the poster to convey.

FIGURE 9

In the general sense, the history of contemporary graphic art has been completely moulded by the course of fine art. The function of the artist includes the invention of new means·of expression and in the last fifty years Picasso has affected the history of modern art as has no other single man.

It has been argued that although Picasso (Cubist), Braque (Cubist), Chagall (Surrealist), Léger (Cubist-Abstract), Matisse (Fauve), Kandinsky (Abstract-Expressionist), and others exerted strong influences on poster design, yet the posters executed by these men themselves do not function effectively as posters. This is the kind of accusation that can produce a plethora of arguments for either side. If by poster is meant the strictly commercial poster designed to sell shoes or sealing wax on a national scale, in small communities as well as in large metropolitan centers, there might be some justice in this criticism. It might be less true of France, where the inhabitants of even the small communities know the names and sometimes the work of these leading artists.

I can easily conceive of the reaction to a Picasso poster in a small or medium-sized community in countries where his work is unknown and consequently not understood. Such a poster would not only not sell shoes, but might even conceivably prejudice the community *against* the shoes. What we don't understand we ridicule and resent.

But this, of course, is a silly argument. The posters of these men are designed for a specific purpose, mostly to advertise exhibits of their own work, and as such are closely identified with the general body of their work. Indeed, to go a step further, one can argue that the posters of these fine artists function in a completely effective way even when submitted to the general test. Can anyone deny the widespread publicity given to the town of Vallauris by the Picasso pottery, ceramic, and bullfight posters? There are very few tourists who have traveled through France during the Easter season who do not know of the Vence Festival of Flowers through Chagall's posters, or of festivals in

FIGURE 10

Cannes and other Riviera spots through those of Matisse and Dufy, or of exhibits at the Galerie Maeght through the posters of Braque, Chagall, and Miró. People familiar with the art world know Henry Kahnweiler as the long-time friend and dealer of Picasso's, but the name of his gallery — The Galerie Lereis — is known only through the posters of Picasso, Léger, and Villon. Maison de la Pensée Française, another exhibition hall, is known in good measure through the poster work of Picasso, Braque, Léger, Matisse, and others.

There is, of course, more to say on the subject. Picasso, Léger, Chagall, Miró, Matisse, and the rest design posters in the genre of their painting. Not only posters, but book jackets also bear the unmistakable stamp of the artist's aesthetic physiognomy. This was as true for Daumier, Delacroix, Lautrec, Fantin-Latour, Bonnard, and Monet as it is for contemporaries. A fine artist can only function within the framework of his own vision, his taste and perception. His taste and perception may change (there is no better example than that offered by Picasso, who went from the Blue Period to the Rose Period to the various Cubist stages to the Classic and neo-Classic, etc.) in which case his work will bear the mark of his changing ideas; but his graphic work will always reflect the period he is working in.

Looked at from still another point of view, it is both unfair and unintelligent to judge present-day posters by the successful poster techniques of the past. It is axiomatic that different periods in history bring different changes in taste. Successful as Lautrec was, I doubt that a current artist working in his outlines would be successful today, any more than a Picasso working in Lautrec's day would have been successful. Each age has its own idiom of art as well as of language; any other is a foreign or historic curiosity. It is true that the ages overlap and each period has parts of the past within it, yet I doubt if a poster artist, except for the "cute" or "chi-chi" trade, could produce successful posters created in the Victorian tradition or even in that of the early twentieth century.

Picasso has had his detractors, no less in his posters than in his fine art. If anything, his posters have come under even greater fire. Because of his extreme simplification, the phrase "My little boy can do better..." is heard even more frequently in this connection. If Picasso has been accused of pulling the leg of the public, his posters convince these critics that their accusation is all the more justified. The unsophisticated observer, brought up and conditioned to believe in an over-elaboration of detail, conventionally composed, as the only true art, rarely appreciates the simple design. He has been thoroughly saturated with the traditional point of view. It is one that he understands and has been disciplined to accept, and he scoffs at the slightest deviation from it.

He therefore sees no reason why any artist should be honored for these uninhibited distortions of his "reality," let alone be paid for it.

Picasso drew his first poster when he was about nineteen in Barcelona *(Figure 11)*. In his treatment of the figures and in the general composition, it is a fairly competent but undistinguished effort. In this poster, he reveals no indication of a powerful and original personality. Although it shows a group of habitués at the Els Quatre Gats Café, there is nothing of the café or its atmosphere in the picture. He signs his name with a P enclosed in a circle after the manner of

the Lautrec signature. But although this poster and his painting of this period both show scarcely any originality, they do possess an unbelievable skill. They show a grasp of fundamentals and a mastery of composition rare in a man of his years. The Picasso touch, however, is yet to emerge.

He did not begin to design posters in any substantial way until 1948 and he did so only in connection with his first poster commissions in Vallauris. There had been posters advertising his works before this but they were not designed by him nor was he consulted in their execution. It is therefore accurate to say that Picasso has been designing posters only for the last ten years. Although they contain elements reflective of all his periods of painting, they do not represent as a totality, in any given single work, his Blue Period or Rose Period or "Girl in the Mirror" period or his Cubist or any other definitive period. These landmarks of his career are deliberately omitted for two reasons: one, he was beyond experimentation in these developments when he began to design posters, and two, he never goes back to a complete part of his past when he is finished with it. Again, he wishes to reduce to a final expression of simplicity this most elementary art of communication. Many of his posters advertise his ceramic exhibits at Vallauris. His plates, vases, and jugs are either in the shape of animals or are decorated with them. Consequently, the posters carry the lettering and a simple sketch of the animals with which his ceramics are identified. His two bullfight posters contain the familiar elements of the bull fight, simply presented in one case as a montage of bull, spectators, and toreador, in the other as a synthesis of bull and picador. His peace poster presents simply the dove, which he has utilized as the symbol of peace.

He uses color sparingly, since color as an element of design contributes to the meaning of the matter advertised. His color in the case of the toros, or bulls, defines the holiday spirit of the arena. The ceramic posters are mostly in one or two colors, as are the ceramics themselves for the most part. Thus, the integration of color and design is carefully worked out.

The truism that the total personality of the man sums up the totality of the artist was never truer than in the case of Picasso. His nervous energy, his boundless curiosity and intellectual capacity, his restlessness, his warm humanity, generosity, friendliness, easy laughter and encompassing sense of humor, his hatred of brutality and paradoxical fascination with cruelty, his love of objects, his

ES-SERVEIX-BEURE-Y-MENJAR-A-TOTES-HORES

·CARRER D
MONTESIÓN·

PERE ROMEU –4 GATS

FIGURE 11

need to work constantly, at any and every form of graphic or plastic expression — these qualities show up again and again in his works.

This applies as much to his posters as it does to any aspect of his creativeness. Picasso, it is true, is not a prolific poster artist. But the posters reproduced in this book are as much Picasso as anything he ever did. The Picasso signature is there — his perception, his humor, his deft and certain touch, his inventiveness. Nobody else could have done these posters exactly this way.

Between the time of designing his first poster and the body of his poster work, some forty-five years later, Picasso has sprung from obscurity into the position of being regarded the world's leading painter. He has become an international personality who has had as much written about him as the head of a large modern state. He has been the center of more controversy than any other artist in the history of painting. His work has been rejected or praised in superlative terms only, and he has left his stamp and personality on the entire body of modern art.

Many of his friends believe that he could have become just as easily a poet, a writer, a film director, or almost anything that requires the free play of the creative spirit. But his painting was put before him when he was scarcely old enough to walk. He was surrounded by painters and sculptors from infancy. His father was a painter of what Picasso called dining-room art (themes of pigeons and fowl), and his friends included painters of Málaga, Barcelona, and Madrid. Picasso was already adept with pencil and crayon at the age of seven, and by the time he had reached double these years his father turned over to him all his brushes,

as though in recognition of his son's superior talent. When he was fifteen, he passed with flying colors the entrance requirements for a class of "advanced modeling and painting." The usual requirement in this class was at least a month's preparation, but Picasso "boned up" in just one day and took honors with ease against adult competition. At the same time he won an honorable mention in an exhibit in Madrid, and a short time later a third prize medal. Some two years later, he gained entrance to an art school in Madrid with the same ease and display of superiority. Thus he manifested quite early in his career a mastery of academic craftsmanship and composition that gave him a distinguished position in art circles of Barcelona and Madrid. But not long after, he turned his back on the conventional techniques. He felt that as his personality — that is, his personal vision — differed from that of other artists, he had to find a method different from theirs to express himself. To do so successfully, he studied all existing techniques and modes of construction, since he felt that a definite relationship existed between the original idea and the manner in which it is expressed. Once he understood this relationship through the various historic examples, he was able to destroy the domination of these historically established techniques, and to create and develop his own.

He also felt that it was important to know inside and out the subject one painted. All people wear a mask, and to paint a human figure without penetrating beyond it was to fail as an artist. The object of the artist was to present the essence, not the appearance. In connection with this he once said, "What is the use of disguise and artificialities in a work of art? What counts is what is impulsive, spontaneous. That is the truthful truth. What we impose on ourselves does not emanate from ourselves." (*Picasso: An Intimate Portrait* by Jaime Sabartes)

He further believes that art is composed of vision and sentiment, and that beauty is a matter of local convention. The cannibal belle with a ring in her nose sets one kind of standard, the Hollywood queen another. But the artist cannot be guided by convention. He must examine and probe and find his own conclusions. "The Renaissance invented the size of noses. Since then reality has gone to the devil," he says.

The search for the proper means to express his own reality led him to Paris. As Sabartes, his secretary, man Friday, and constant companion, put it, "Art, like dressmaking, had to cross the

Pyrenees in order to get established."

Between 1900 and 1904 he made four trips to Paris, where he lived for varying periods of time. Finally in 1904 he settled in Paris for good. He brought with him feelings of sadness and pain, derived from his first-hand experience with poverty, grief, and loneliness. In fact, so imbued was he with these feelings that he felt that art could be born only of misery and poverty. From this period came his Blue paintings, with their emaciated, hopeless, lost figures. This attitude was altered somewhat by the air of Paris, and the Blue began to give way to the Rose Period. The figures are now pensive, graceful, and no longer lost. They belong to the world of the circus — tumblers, acrobats, clowns, and the like — and are part of a profession. Now, although they are still often sad, they are no longer abandoned. But the technique that was to answer his searchings he finally found in Cubism, which was introduced to the world by the now famous "Les Desmoiselles d'Avignon." This painting marked the turning point, both in his career and in modern art. With it he broke with tradition, turning his back on all previously proven techniques. His capacity for work, his tenacity — for which he was noted — stood him in good stead. He made no less than seventeen different interpretations of this work, to say nothing of the countless drawings of the individual figures in the composition. It was a lonely path, but Picasso took it without hesitation. His probings and investigations turned up a "nose" with a different size. This was the direction that his vision demanded.

When he was finished with Cubism, he was only twenty-five. While most artists of that age and older were still struggling with basic problems of technique and a workable apparatus of expression Picasso had gone through three major periods, evolved a technique that was to transform modern art, and produced an unbelievable amount of work. Although he was still unknown to the public, he had by this time completed no less than two hundred paintings in oil, water color, and gouache, and unknown numbers of charcoal, pen and pencil, and crayon drawings, as well as lithographs, dry point etchings, woodcuts, scultpures, to say nothing of the vast numbers of water colors and drawings he had burned up in the stove as fuel during the bitterest stretches of his poverty-ridden days, about the winter of 1904.

In the course of his artistic life, Picasso has concluded that a painter must have four things:

intelligence, memory, sensibilities or the free play of the senses, and energy and tenacity — meaning of course, that he has found that he needs these qualities at all times to solve his own problems. To American painters who have gone to him for advice over the years, he has always advised work and patience. He himself has no patience, but he makes up for this lack with a tireless persistence.

For all his uncompromising pursuit of objectives and for all his maverick defiances and his disregard for popular approval, Picasso is a sentimentalist with a strong attachment for family. He has brothers, sisters, uncles, and aunts in profusion, and although he never or almost never writes to them, he is conscious of his clan affiliations. He comes from a strong Catholic background and was baptized with eight Christian names, beginning with Pablo and ending with Cuspiniano de la Santissima Trinidad. He never allows sentimentality to gain control and divert the main direction of his life, but he does keep among his souvenirs a complete album of photographs of all his kin, and he treasures the various iconographies of his family tree. And for all his more than fifty years of uninterrupted living in France, he is still said to be more Spanish than French. (Gertrude Stein once told him that Cubism was a visual interpretation of Spanish landscapes.)

There is a story going the rounds, probably apocryphal, to illustrate his sentimental attachment for the old country. While on a visit to Picasso, an art collector and old friend of the painter, who fancied himself a culinary artist, agreed to prepare a fine meal. Picasso invited about eight people and the amateur chef got busy. After some three hours in the kitchen, punctuated by pounding, grinding, and chopping noises, and running in and out by Inez, the *femme de ménage*, with various items of kitchenware from her own kitchen below, the chef finally bore to the table in great triumph a fine rendition of chicken suprême, garnished with pommes Dauphine, peas Provençal, and whole-cranberry sauce. The last item the collector had brought from America. Picasso tasted the cranberries, liked them, and asked for more. When he finished the second helping, he asked for still more. Finally he asked for the rest of the can and subsequently did away with half of a second one. All the while, he never touched any of the chicken or the other dishes that the friend had labored so heroically to create. While the latter puzzled over this inordinate taste for the cranberries, one of the diners explained, "Although the chicken is excellent, it does not tempt him. He has good French food all the time, but the cranberries—that is another matter. They are not too plentiful in Paris and they remind him of Spain."

Picasso is now in his seventy-sixth year but he still possesses an incredible stamina. He likes to show off his firm torso, his sturdy, well-modeled, strong legs. His physical attributes he regards as a practical necessity, the essentials that provide power for his intense work-days. At the age of sixty-five, after a career that would serve to satisfy a dozen painters, Picasso donned workman's clothes, went into the shop of the Medoura ceramic studios, and in an amazingly short time emerged as the master of a new craft. After one year, he had produced over two thousand pieces, and his exhibit of over 160 pieces at the Maison Française in Paris was the talk of the ceramics world. Within two years he had transformed the entire pottery industry and Vallauris became a world pottery center. Needless to say, every potter in Vallauris now shows the Picasso influence in his work.

But whether it be ceramics, paintings, drawing, sculpture, posters, or any other mode of expression, all his work bears the hallmark of his creativity, his incisive touch. The creative act is often entangled in uncertainty. It is hedged with false starts, erasures, rejections, and the like. But not so with Picasso. Once his course is decided upon, he proceeds from beginning to end with swift, sure, unhesitating strokes. The total image or end product is fixed in his mind beforehand. It is as though he possessed a photographic memory of something yet to be born. This was apparent in the film *Le Mystére de Picasso*. Clouzot, the director, was aware of this quality and gave Picasso a free hand in the making of the film. The use of a chemically treated canvas made it possible to photograph Picasso at work from its reverse side. The viewer see his pencil or brush at work, but sees him only when he emerges from behind the canvas. We are, in effect, seeing him at work as he would be when alone. The brush moves rapidly over the areas of the canvas. He pauses from time to time to study the result. If it is not to his liking, he mutters *"Mal, mal,"* and starts afresh. If the thing goes wrong, that is if the work of his hand does not conform to his vision of the idea, he starts anew. Erasures, chicken scratching, wiping, and repainting are not part of his technique. Several times he puts his brush in the middle of the canvas, that is to say, somewhere in the middle of his composition, and then swiftly completes the picture, moving in all directions without hesitation. This might be regarded as a trick, something thought up to amuse movie audiences. While it is true that this is not a usual method of procedure, and while it is also true that it might be regarded as a sort of artistic lagniappe for the spectator, it is rather an expression of a degree of technique. For this is meant to demonstrate the certainty of his touch, his assurance in knowing what he is going after. A spectator was once heard to say that Picasso probably did that particular composition so often that he knew where each line went, and that he could consequently paint and draw it backwards, sideways, up and down from sheer memory. Such an assumption is not unreasonable, yet it is completely untrue. A film made in Italy showed Picasso taking a piece of raw clay and, in an instant, molding and shaping a figure he had never done before. Sabartes, in discussing this film with friends, said that that spot was the high moment in the entire film, since it showed Picasso in the unpremeditated creative act. Sabartes, who has been with Picasso since their early Barcelona days more than fifty years ago, is constantly surprised by Picasso's creative agility.

This quality is matched by an unquenchable curiosity. His studio is a catch-all of old posters, decals, ancient lithographs, fine paintings, drawings, prints of every description. I was surprised to discover old genre cliché paintings, sentimental buckeyes of every clime and time. When I expressed surprise over his collecting them, he explained that everything painted or drawn had something of interest if not of value.

He is deeply interested in every form of printmaking and he has tried them all—etching, carving, gouging, dry point, stone lithography. As a result of this interest, he has produced work in almost every form of expression, on every type of surface, in every known medium — drawing, aquatint, sculpture, oil, water color, pen and ink, charcoal, crayon, pastel, lithograph — producing work in enormous quantities. An exhibit at the Museum of Modern Art in New York commemorating his seventy-fifth birthday showed works on four floors. Because of limited space the exhibit was confined largely to oils and drawings. There is only one known medium of the graphic art that he has not yet tried. This is the animated film and the only reason he has not done so, he says, is because it is not up to him. The machinery of producing his drawings in animation is beyond his knowledge or means, but he says he is most willing to try it.

He does not wait for "inspiration." He is never at a loss for something to paint or draw or mould.

It accounts for his interminable curiosity, his ever-present restlessness. While he talks to someone, his eyes are never still. He watches the other's face, his eyes, lips, hands, movements — not obtrusively, so as to make him self-conscious or interfere with the conversation or argument, but nothing escapes him. His son Claude has the same restless eyes, the same curiosity, the same interest in people. When visitors indicate that they are aware of this trait in his son, he is extremely pleased.

Picasso's hands, too, are rarely still. He picks up anything within reach, a pencil, a piece of clay or wire, a ball of dried rubber cement, and he begins to mould shapes or draw. His hands work as he talks and soon you begin to appreciate the degree of his plastic or graphic facility. His zeal, his energy, his urge to work, his need to make something out of the raw products of his craft are as strong as ever. He combines the experience of half a century with the avidity of youth.

To create in life is, of course, to love life and all forms of living. From early childhood he has been interested in owls, monkeys, goats, bulls, pigeons, turtles. He has kept all sorts of animals in his studio, both as models and as interesting examples of animal behavior. The owl, the bull, the pigeon or dove, have always served as symbols for him and as such are present in much of his work. The bull (in the arena) is the challenge, the brutish charge that is met with courage, skill and grace. The dove is tenderness, the antithesis of inhumanity. The owl is the mystery, the being that neither demands nor gives, that calls derisively out of the dark, that keeps its own counsel and seemingly mocks at all our ambitions and agitations.

Conversely, he abhors all destruction of life. He has made no secret of his opposition to Franco, Hitler, and war. Although he makes the bull the symbol of fascist brutality, he does not hate the bull in itself, nor any form of unpremeditated cruelty in nature, since that cruelty exists as an impulse in the structure of self-preservation. He opposes only the calculated, needless slaughter that war and tyranny impose on nations and individuals.

In a way, one can say that his love of life is at the bottom of his aesthetic impulses. It shapes the attitudes, the method of looking at things, the inner and outer vision or manner of examining and interpreting physical and emotional phenomena. Although he understands the impulses that determine the behavior of things natural, he has no wish as an artist to be bound hand and foot by

nature. From the days when he began making his own path, his aim was to free himself from the tyranny of nature, and of perspective, the conventional way of apprehending reality and nature. He had first to destroy the forms of nature before he could create in his own terms. This way of looking at things, this vision, led to Cubism, to the "Girl in the Mirror" period, his probing investigations of the human form, his imposition of angles upon angles of the human face in order to present aspects of human features not previously examined or exposed. The results were often rejected by everybody except those close to him or his steadfast appreciators. He has been called a distorter of the human figure, an artist who invested his work with hideous disfigurations, or with abstruse meanings. To all of this he shrugs his shoulders. Nobody ever called Maxfield Parrish a distorter of nature or of the human figure; no slick magazine illustrators such as the Rockwells, Flaggs, or their European equivalents, were ever the center of any significant controversy. His objectives do not include a bid for popularity; he has never wanted to be a matinée idol of art. He could have continued in the vein of his Blue and Rose periods and thus avoided all controversy. But he is essentially an artist, forever posing problems which he tackles with a vigor and honesty as rare as his talent. He may not have succeeded in solving a particular problem to his ultimate satisfaction, but he worked at it until he could bring no more to it. Once finished, he never returned to it. Thus he has constantly gone on to new ideas, creating new periods of work, new styles of interpretation. Had he wanted what most painters want — critical recognition and public success, he could have stopped at Cubism, at his classical periods, or at any point along the way that met with public satisfaction and approval.

He has been accused of pulling the legs of people, of clowning, or smirkingly passing off a gaffe upon an unsuspecting buyer. This, of course, is arrant nonsense. He could no more sell a painting as a trick upon a buyer than we could scotch our Supreme Court. What is true is that he has a sly and often devastating sense of humor. He feels uncomfortable in an atmosphere of stuffiness. He likes to deflate pomposity or to avert a situation that threatens to become unnecessarily or unjustifiably serious. Recently a prominent textile firm conducted a national promotion campaign featuring the designs of Picasso, Miró, Braque, Chagall, Léger and others. *Life* magazine photographed the artists with models dressed in material bearing their designs. On the surface all the artists were serious, as was to be expected; but Picasso appeared in shorts, wearing a fedora and carrying a saber, in ludicrous contrast to the elegant model posing with him. When the film, *Le Mystère de Picasso,* won a prize at the Cannes Film Festival of 1956, he made a concession to the formality of the evening by appearing in a tuxedo and derby hat at least twenty years old, and as Sabartes declared, of an interesting green color.

It is his way of letting people know that although he will participate in the mumbo-jumbo of formality or in the straight-faced dignity of big business, he will not be taken in by it.

Not all his humor is barbed. It is just as frequently warm and friendly and playful. One year I brought "fur hats," of the kind worn by Westchester motorcycle policemen, to both himself and Sabartes. The next day he greeted me at the door, wearing the hat, brandishing a pistol, and doing a war dance. It turned out that he identified the hat with fur trappers and the trappers with Indians. Once he was talking to an American collector and wound up the conversation with "O.K." The collector in an attempt to be humorous said, "Ah, you talk English — where did you learn it?" and quick as a flash Picasso replied, "From you."

Upon returning late from a party he once left this note for Sabartes: "It is now two o'clock in the morning of the ninth day of the year MCMXXXI. Sabartes, you who know personally each and every hour, ask eight-thirty to leap into my bed and awaken me."

Some time later, in Nice, writing to Sabartes in Paris, he said, "I am writing you immediately to inform you that as of this afternoon, I am giving up painting, sculpture, engraving, and poetry in order to devote myself exclusively to singing." (Both letters from *Picasso: An Intimate Portrait*)

Although Picasso has set for himself more problems (as reflected in his changing compositions and periods) than probably any other artist in the history of painting, a distinction that indicates pondering, reflectiveness, careful selection of detail and color, he is as spontaneous and eruptive as he is deliberate. He apparently makes up his mind with great rapidity and then executes his ideas with a burst of nonstop energy. Such spontaneity seems deceptive, because what he does requires great discipline and organization. Where the discipline shows in men of smaller talent, you often have laborious and slow progress. Facility, it has been argued, indicates shallowness while slow, deliberate, careful organization is synonymous with

profundity; but Picasso is the living refutation of this theory, or at least its fiery exception.

He loves children, his own and those of others, with a humanity and warmth that is only to be expected of a man of his outgoing manner. He spends a great deal of time with his children whom he embraces continuously with a great love, and when he is with them he will allow nothing to interfere with these sessions. He showers them with toys which he patiently winds and operates for them, and in general behaves like the most commonplace doting father. It is true that he conducts an irregular or unconventional household, and the children respect and accept the pattern he imposes. He often works far into the night or else takes off without a moment's notice to spend time with the trainers of bulls at the toro farms in Céret, or else goes to Paris, or to the ceramic studios or a half-dozen other places. These are the idiosyncrasies that must be allowed him or any other painter who can only work in his own time and in his own way.

He is, moreover, extremely generous with his time and help. His aid to indigent friends and associates is by now history. He gives of his time freely. When a young relative of the owner of the ceramic studio he uses was recently married, he decorated the apartment of the newlyweds with murals. He has singlehandedly supported hospitals in France and has given large sums to miners out of work. Although he earns huge sums, he does not live in the manner defined by wealth. He bought a large estate at Cannes last year only because he had never, as he put it, had sufficient place to work, to spread his canvases and note the progression of his work.

He sets aside a certain number of hours each day for visitors, students, and friends. No student is so humble that Picasso will not listen to his problem and discuss it with him. I have visited the studios of Léger, Miró, Chagall, Braque — all men of social habits who do not mind spending time talking with young painters — but I have never seen a stream of art students anywhere to equal the numbers that besiege Picasso daily. The only reason he confines these visits to specified hours is that if he didn't, he would never get any work done at all.

In short, his personal life is a summary of his total art personality and the one cannot be separated from the other. To do so would be to fail to understand either. In bringing up his personal life, his detractors invariably mention what they consider his scandalous record with women. Perhaps by some conventional standards he might be placed among the irresponsible playboys of the world. But he is not a conventional man and his relations with women are never trivial or flippant. His complete life is the full life of the senses and a woman, in the ideal and biblical sense, is as necessary to Picasso as paints and canvas. A man of his warmth needs companionship as constantly as he needs to work. Both are necessary for the fulfillment of his ego. There have been other artists with the same total needs. In recent art history, we have, for instance, Van Gogh and Gauguin. But Van Gogh was blocked and frustrated by neuroses and a misdirection of energy from which he never recovered, the ever-pressing need for fulfillment finally creating the conditions for ultimate madness and suicide. Gauguin also was driven by such need for fulfillment, and he too was blocked, first by social forces and then by a family circle that could not understand his needs and his drives. He had more objectivity than Van Gogh and he went far from home, from the forces that hindered him, to seek some unity between his being and achieving. Unlike Picasso, however, he never succeeded in establishing order and discipline in his life.

The completely realized personality of Picasso, as fully dedicated to his calling as the most dedicated priest in the Catholic hierarchy, is reflected in the total output of the artist, of which the posters are a definitely recognizable part. The steady simplification of line from Lautrec to the present finds its apotheosis in Picasso. He has, together with Matisse, the most highly developed maquette — that is, the number of lines necessary to complete a drawing. Their drawing is often done in one stroke, one continuous line. It is not to be construed that such economy of rendition is always satisfactory to the artist. Picasso made thousands of drawings before he was satisfied with the one that was to guide him in the sculpture of his celebrated "Man Holding a Sheep." Often too, a complicated drawing with full shading is necessary to render the subject properly. But the important thing is that when a few strokes of the pencil are all that is needed, these artists are capable of producing masterful results in this technique.

THE PLATES

Plate 1.

This poster was the first of two on the same subject executed by the artist and his first commission from the town of Vallauris. Specializing in ceramics, flowers, and perfumes, but especially the first, the community arranged its first organized postwar effort to call the attention of the world, tourist and domestic, to its special wares. Picasso composed his poster in two ways. In the first, his treatment is relatively traditional, with flat areas arranged in what is, for this artist, an almost symmetrical style. But Picasso has always fought symmetry, and even in this relatively conventional treatment he introduced variations and inventions to take the curse off it. For instance, over the white ovals of the eyes, nose, and mouth and those around the circumference, he imposes a second black linear oval, thus creating a variety of shapes and forms. In the lower righthand corner, he omits this black linear oval, in order to break up the symmetry of his own invention.

Plate 2.

In this second treatment of the same subject, he departs from the flat area treatment of the first poster by introducing a textural quality. This is more characteristic of Picasso's general technique, the use of texture to obtain an extra excitement — what in music is called vibrato. Here too he eschews symmetry but he does it not only by introducing the wood-grain effect on the surface, but also by splitting the composition into brown and white to create the illusion of two planes on the same surface. Notice also his treatment of the eyes and horns. The shapes of the eyes differ from one another; but he restores whatever imbalance is thus created by varying the shapes of the pupils and the brown areas around them. In a similar manner, the brown area of the right horn dips below the defining line of the shape, while the brown area of the left horn stops above the line. In this manner, he maintains a constant relationship of white to brown area but never in the same way. The black defining line is also drawn asymmetrically. As Joseph Solman, the American painter, once put it, "There are two types of trolley rides, one smooth and uneventful, during which I invariably go to sleep. Then there is the second kind in which the trolley careens along, threatening to go off the track but never does. This second ride is full of suspense and excitement. You know you will arrive right side up, but the sensations vary from moment to moment. When I look at this poster, I get that kind of a ride."

Plate 3.

This is the first of a series of posters that Picasso designed for his own ceramic exhibits. Of extremely simple design, it is one of the most inventive and subtle posters he has ever made. To begin with, the continuous circular line forming concentric circles is an historic design found on ancient pottery of Latin America. What could be more suitable than its use to advertise a ceramic and pottery show? Then by the deft use of a few dots, circles, and lines, he transforms this design into the face of an owl, one of his own design motifs. This is invention on a high level indeed. Here, too, the letters form an integral part of design. Cleverly cut into a variety of shapes and forms, they have the weight of block letters. The hand-cut lettering also provides a dramatic contrast to the mechanical type faces of the rest of the lettering. The over-all design of the composition, with the heavy brown area to compensate for the drawing of the upper part, makes for balance and easy readability. This work, with its deceptive simplicity, demonstrates with what effortless technique Picasso brings off a complex effect.

Plate 4.

Here again Picasso presents two versions of the same subject. In this first treatment of the satyr, another of his favorite ceramic decorations, he creates a calligraphic effect. But the quality of the line he wants to get is best achieved by printing from blocks. Here he uses the gouging tool with the same sureness of touch that characterizes his brush and pen strokes. Again he demonstrates his war on symmetry. The face is composed roughly of three areas, all differing in form. Each eye is treated in characteristic fashion, i.e., the differences are compensated for by the variation of the shapes of the areas of which they are the center. The mouth is drawn thin at one end and thick at the other, the thick end under the narrow area, the thin end under the broad. The bottom area is likewise bound by a line that goes from thin to thick, that begins under the line of the left section and finishes up beyond this line into open space on the right. These inventive touches, all calculated to create varying forms within a framework of over-all simplicity are arrived at almost intuitively, and are invariably right. This of course, is the measure of the artist. If his intuition is unsound, he will inevitably fail.

Plate 5.

In the second treatment of this subject, composed of the same three basic areas, the calligraphic treatment gives way to the illusion of a scupltured mass. The satyr's head now fills the space with a bold massive feeling. The head is invested with ears, additional head structure, eyebrows, and neck. Again he uses the gouging tool with the same ease to produce the effects he wants. Eyebrows, ears, and neck are given the same asymmetric treatment and compensatory balance. But in this instance he resorts to a bit of symmetry to maintain the over-all balance. In general, symmetry in design is deadening since it pulls the eye somewhere toward the center of the design, where it remains. By breaking up this evenness, the eye is released to travel to all sections of a composition. If the artist is inventive and original, then the eye will find freshness and interest wherever it rests. In an inferior artist, this need to break up the monotony of symmetry can lead to a lack of balance and to subsequent collapse. That is to say, unless each work maintains an equilibrium, it will fail. In this instance, the heavily shaded areas create an imbalance that Picasso restores by the addition of the symmetrical head planes, wittily surmounted at dead center by the numerals 1955. He does not fear the result of this evenness at the top, since there is a sufficiency of variety and asymmetry throughout to create interest and to maintain it.

Plate 6.

In this poster, Picasso introduces a complete change of pace. On this occasion, the poster was designed to advertise a series of lithographs created by Picasso for the book *The Chant of the Dead* by Pierre Reverdy. In this work, he composes his effect in stark, simple terms — the figure of a dog, the symbol of a sorrowing friend—drawn in the most intense color of the spectrum against a white background. The lettering in reduced block type emphasizes the simplicity of design and the drama of the announcement. This poster was exhibited in the San Francisco Art Museum.

Plate 7.

This poster, I believe, is the only one demonstrating the use of *papier collé* by Picasso. This technique has been attributed by most critics to his period of "Synthetic Cubism," the chief characteristic of which is the synthesizing of the Cubist with the traditional, or classic, technique. *Papier collé,* within this framework, contrasts the abstract design of a composition against the full and conventional details of the paper paste-up. The newspaper is used as a sort of reminder of reality, while the artist exercises his full imagination in the realm of the abstract. In this poster, the small rectangular paper cut-out functions in this manner. The heavy red border serves to separate the elements of the poster illustration from the lettering so as to achieve the maximum effectiveness of the *papier collé* idea.

Plate 8.

There are many touches both of interest and of humor in this placard. Dominant in this design are the overlapping or interpenetrating planes characteristic of Cubism. This is not to say that the work is rendered in the total Cubist technique. It has been said, and rightly, that once Picasso has made a complete investigation into a theory or an idea, he leaves it never to return. However, it is equally true that he never relinquishes any of the discoveries or developments that have come from such investigations. Consequently, although he has never returned to Cubism as a total form of painting, Cubist ideas, influences, and touches appear subsequently in his works. With regard to the poster, it is therefore not surprising to find the overlapping planes of Cubism providing an incomparable richness and inventiveness. The two planes of the single surface are furnished by the black ink on the coral-colored paper. The gouging tool does the rest. Both coral-colored paper and black ink areas, by their action one against the other, take turns serving both as foreground and background. The horns and the lettering carry out this interpenetration. The top lettering appears to be gouged against a black background but the second half of the Vallauris lettering alters the accent of the background as do the horns in relation to each other. This technique provides a movement, depth, and variety obtainable only by the use of Cubist techniques. In addition, the lettering is cleverly used to emphasize the goatish quality of the design. Wherever possible, the letter ends in sharp points to suggest the horns and thus create a unity between lettering and illustration. Picasso also adds a characteristic touch of humor by drawing the first "O" in the shape of the sun. Since all the

commercial agencies of the Riviera sell the sun as their chief attraction, Picasso indulges in a slight spoof by surrounding 1952 with the symbol of this playground of the South.

Plate 9.

In the Vallauris exposition poster of 1954, the same technique of interpenetrating planes is observable. Here, too, the gouging tool is his instrument of execution, and he cleverly works in the green and black tones so that each serves as background and foreground in overlapping effects, thus creating an illusion of depth on the single surface without resorting to the use of perspective. An additional characteristic of Cubism is the manner in which he draws in the shadow-lines of the green vase on the black, thus providing added variety of forms. He also boldly draws lines across the base and the neck of the vases to create interesting shapes that counterbalance the roundness of the sides. Thus in the process of integrating one vase within the shape of the other, he produces form within form in endless variety. The shooting lines of white on black, and green on black help the overlapping action and at the same time provide the additional excitement that is so characteristic of Picasso's textural inventiveness.

Plate 10.

This poster was commissioned by the city of Nice for its annual carnival. Here the figure is one of a happy jovial king, the traditional symbol by which Nice introduces the carnival and advertises itself as a gay holiday resort. The colors are bright and direct, emphasizing the gala spirit of the community. In this particular poster Picasso exchanges the gouging tool for a flat stub pen as the best tool for controlling the rhythm of line. This rhythm is obtained by varying the width of the stroke. This is especially noticeable in the center of the face and in the upstrokes of the wavy border lines. He knows exactly what is going to develop as, with an easy, unfaltering movement, he starts the composition at the center (in the area of the nose) and in one unending line completes the face. Notice, too, how he encloses one eye and puts the other in open space. One ear is closed, one open. The right side of the crown is open, the left closed, etc. The three sides of the border are yellow with blue and red dots, the top border simply blue. Three rows of black, i.e., the eyes, the nostrils, the ruff, while differing in length from each other, create a feeling of balance for the face that otherwise would be floating in space. All these touches, while seemingly casual, are carefully thought out to provide interest, solidity, variety, and movement—touches that the Picasso follower now takes for granted.

Plate 11.

The 1953 Vallauris poster is not typical of Picasso's general work; yet once observed, it is found to be neither strange nor alien to his thinking. In this instance, although he uses the figures as in a movie close-up, his main effects are so arranged as to emphasize the sun of the Riviera, that eternal beacon of *tourisme*. He makes the figures bold to emphasize their importance, a purpose easy to understand since they represent his two children and Françoise — his inamorata of that time. The green, red, yellow bands of colors, creating the effect of an abstract-impressionist sky, saves the design from classic banality. The word "effect" is used advisedly in relation to "sky" because although the feeling of sky is not accidental, the brilliant bands of color are used as something more, mainly as a full background with a design of its own, carried out from green band on top to green band on bottom, and is meant to encompass the total poster, including the lettering, and to provide a unity of balance between top and bottom.

Plate 12.

This poster is composed of three distinct elements: the hand-lettered block name running the full length of the poster on the left and printed in reverse, the painting in the upper righthand area, and the Japanese lettering below it. Here Picasso illustrates the truism that nothing is as deadly as an unchangable rule. Although, as he demonstrates time and again, the symmetrical design is pallid, in this particular instance the block lettering must be kept more or less in symmetry. Where normally he would have used a variety of shapes in the lettering, to do so in this poster would have created a chaos of movement. The Japanese lettering adjacent to it, by its characteristics, provides the differentiation he normally seeks. Since the foreign lettering is a constant and fills a practical need, he must give way to it. The block lettering running the full length of the poster ties the other two elements together.

Plate 13.

This poster was designed for his huge and important "War and Peace" exhibit held in Milan in 1955. This poster, the only original one designed in connection with the exhibit, illustrated the section of the show dealing with war. His object is to depict its horrors, with all its agonized and dramatic impact. This effect is admirably achieved by the few simple heavy red lines drawn sharply against the dark background. The position of the face and arm, the tensed, outstretched fingers, reveal in powerful and unmistakable terms the anguish and tension that harass people caught in the horrors of war. The broken blue line at the bottom of the drawing anchors the figure and also provides the characteristic textural touch. The stark simplicity of his drawing is demonstrated by the one line on the left forming the arm, the chin, and the outline of the face.

Plate 14.

Here the artist takes a small journey into the past. This is a traditional lithograph, done on stone and imbued with the soft poetic quality that the stone surface, properly used, can produce so well. In keeping with the gentle and subtle qualities of his colorings, the composition is arranged in classical style. The lettering maintains the softness through the use of the textured background and becomes by this device an integral part of the design. The owl, an ever-recurring trademark in both his posters and other forms of Picasso's art, is particularly appropriate because this bird is for him a symbol of subtlety. It also, by its shape, furnishes a roundness that is in keeping with the tone of the design.

Plate 15.

The drawing technique of this poster is related to the "nervous" muscular touch that was characteristic of his bulls and minotaurs of the thirties. It serves as an interesting contrast to the calligraphic style of *Plate 19*, a forerunner of the style used in his *Comédie Humaine* drawings. The lettering is designed in the same style. The theme of the drawing demonstrates his delicious humor, his satirical thrust at traditional institutions. The three figures are composed of two men shaking a tambourine while each holds the hand of a girl between them. The drawing and the treatment of the figures provide a rich burlesque of the *Fêtes Galantes,* celebrated by Watteau and others in their fashionable depictions. The *Fêtes Galantes* have been held in esteem throughout a continuous French tradition, and provide an understandable target for his wit. The green and orange-brown lines and the blue scribbles contribute to the background and visual excitement.

Plate 16.

In the Matisse manner, this composition depicts a sweet and gentle face, poetically and evocatively drawn. Here he uses one simple color to maintain the lyrical mood. The design is cleverly worked out so that the lettering and figures blend its elements one into the other. For instance, the figure 1 of 1951 is a definite part of the pattern indicating the hair line above the eyes. The style of the lettering, composed of short thick strokes as in the V, the A, the L, the I, the T, the N, etc, is in keeping with the style of the hairline. The curls on each side of the face are drawn to harmonize with the flower decor. Thus, drawing and lettering and decoration are all integrated.

Plates 17 and 18.

Plates *17* and *18* are more or less conventional treatments of what to Picasso are important subjects. He wished nothing to stand between the message of each poster and a maximum number of readers. Here he functions as the typical poster artist in that he wishes to efface himself as much as possible, to remove any effects that might contend with the message. Of course, *(Plate 17)* the dove can no more be separated from Picasso than Paris from the Champs-Elysées. The dove is selected as his universal symbol of peace and good will, the antithesis of antagonism and warring elements. Since the white color of the dove is fixed by both nature and classical tradition, he surrounds it with black the better to obtain the maximum "whiteness." For similar reasons he uses strong block letters to emphasize the meaning and importance of the poster. In *Plate 18,* the lettering, by contrast, harmonizes with the drawing of the face. Here he wishes to present the poet of the poster with an air

of gentility, and to impart to the whole poster a quality of calm and dignity.

Plate 19.

This is another of his "calligraphic" posters in which he humorously depicts the traditional figures of Don Quixote and Sancho Panza with his own brand of fun. The symbol this time is once again a dove. The lettering has the same quality as the drawing and provides a marvelous unity with it. It is interesting to note that although very often his lettering is deliberately shaped to match the drawing of the poster, he succeeds in obtaining totally different results for each one. Notice, too, how Picasso creates a unity of movement and design by constructing the beard of the righthand face, the fingers of the same figure, and the feathers of the dove in the same style. By drawing the fingers this way, he also gets the additional effect of visual excitement.

Plate 20.

Here is a tricky combination of design and lettering, which incidentally is one of the few posters that has drawn adverse criticism. It is too difficult to read, these critics say, and hence defeats its own practical purpose as a poster. At first glance, this may seem to be so, and would be quite true had it been designed and placed in a spot where people could read only while on the run. Moreover, Picasso feels that by now the Vallauris trademark, like the red, black, and white of the San Rafael wine posters, has become so identified with the subject that normal poster clarity can be sacrificed to ingenuity and playfulness in design. Furthermore, the European tradition and particularly that of the Riviera holds to the belief that people have sufficient time and leisure to study a poster that calls for one's attention. The central motif is the owl. The upward curve of the S and the upper left stroke of the X form the horns. Furthermore, the manner in which the T is shaped and the I dotted form a second face. The O in the center of the X and O of the word "exposition" form the eyes of the bird. But he does not let the matter rest at this point. He extends the design and creates a series of O's throughout, such as in the A, and R, the P, the dotting of the I's, etc. Thus the eyes of the bird become part of the over-all design rather than a cliché. He *uses* the trick, but at once disarms the observer by taking the emphasis away from it. The white circle around the face is drawn more or less evenly and gives it stability. The asymmetry of design in this case is provided by the sharp, uneven thrust of the letters breaking through it. The feeling of roundness and of circularity is provided not only by the central figure but by the treatment of the letters, such as the E, the X, the P, the S, etc.

Plates 21 and 22.

Plates 21 and *22* are the two celebrated bullfight posters created by Picasso for the Vallauris arena. Both are executed in blue, red, and yellow, utilized in brilliant fashion to reflect the holiday spirit. *Plate 21* is the first of these two in which all elements are reduced to a fundamental symbology. The arena is seen through a framework created by a top structure as roof, a girder that splits the frame, and the lower part from where you, as spectator, look out on the field. The girder-divided frame creates the two areas of light and dark: the shadowy stands and the brilliant sun-drenched field. The illusion of light and dark is further heightened by the circle of faces moving out on both sides from the spectator. Each side of the arena is in balance with the other by virtue of the fact that each contains one of the two important figures in the drama of the bullfight. On one side is the toreador who is about to place the banderillos, and on the other the bull. Both appear motionless, creating an instant of overwhelming suspense. It is the moment when the toreador is most vulnerable, without even the protection of the cape, and similarly the moment when the bull has been goaded to the utmost by everything that has gone before. Thus, Picasso picks the climax of the spectacle for his illustration.

In the second of the bullfight posters, the composition is somewhat more complex. It features a construction of pictorial meaning within pictorial meaning, like mirrors reflecting each other. It is a form of construction of which Picasso is fond since it creates an endless variety of forms. The over-all dominating image of the poster is the eye of the bull that fills all the space between the letters. Everything that Picasso wishes to show is reflected in the bull's eye and as such cleverly presents a visual target for the poster spectator. The righthand section depicts the picador on his horse facing the door that leads to the arena. The lefthand side in yellow and red shows the bull ready and waiting. In this section, the eye of the bull is the same shape as the body. The legs and horns are drawn to match the general stroking that obtains throughout. The evenness of the outer defining circle is broken up by the small dabs of paint on the inner and outer side of the line. Noticeable in connection with this treatment is the rough, uneven line of the letters in contrast to the smoothness of the letters in *Plate 21*. In each case there is a unity between the lettering and the circle defining the theme of the poster. In both sections of the bull's eye poster are to be found, once again, the shooting lines which Picasso uses to obtain that extra dimension of feeling.

Plate 23.

This poster advertising the 1952 Vallauris exhibit is easily the most ambitious, the most interesting, and the most powerful of his late Vallauris posters. His circle defining the owl's head is more or less smooth and symmetrical, but here he breaks up the evenness and creates movement and variety by a brilliant use of color. The head is divided into three sections, each differing in treatment from the others. In the two end areas, the eye is presented in profile, yet each is drawn differently from the other. The full face in the center has still a different eye treatment. The center is treated symmetrically and provides the balance for the entire composition, yet because of the variation in treatment and color of the whole, the eye of the spectator never rests on this section only. On the left, the textural lines are outside the face but on the right they are on the face. This variation in color and movement is carried out by the lettering, by unevenness in size and the change of color from red to green.

Plate 24.

This poster is highly complex and includes techniques found in various Picasso periods. The face is again divided into three distinct planes. The eye, all in black, is set in the center of the flat blue area and is matched in design by the black line dividing the face from the rest of the blue area. The eye on the right is so constructed as to carry the white, and if you place your hand to the left of the nose, just covering the left eye, you will notice the profile effect that the face takes on. Remove your hand and the full face emerges again. Thus you have the combination of full face and profile that dominated his work in the forties. The lower part of the composition within the red field is highly reminiscent of that stage of the Cubist period dominated by the famous "Three Musicians." The overlapping of planes, the shifting emphasis of background and foreground is unmistakable. This part of the poster is so complex that very little can be done to the right side. Yet so large an area cannot be left hanging. Picasso solves the problem by breaking up the space with his textural dabs of paint. The figure on the left, the heavy block lettering, and the dabs on the right could very easily produce an impression of overcrowding; but Picasso avoids this by keeping the upper part relatively untouched, by matching the dabs with the strokes on the lower left figure, and by concentrating the activity more or less in the center (achieved by placing the name in heavy block letters toward the center of the poster).

After looking at these twenty-four plates, it is obvious that Picasso, even in this relatively minor field of work is remarkably inventive, facile, and original. Although touches and details are repeated, no two posters are alike. Each poster demands its own laws of unity and in each case he pursues different methods to attain it; the use of color in relation to the content, the relation of the details to each other and of the lettering to the whole.

These varied posters serve admirably to show Picasso's creative range.

POSTERS

EXPOSITION
DU 24 JUILLET AU 29 AOUT
POTERIES
FLEURS
PARFUMS
VALLAURIS
.A.M.

PLATE 1

PLATE 2

POTERIES

PICASSO

de

DU 27 NOVEMBRE 1948
AU 5 JANVIER 1949

à la Maison de la Pensée Française

2, RUE DE L'ÉLYSÉE · PARIS

TOUS LES JOURS DE 10 HEURES À MIDI ET DE 14 À 19 HEURES

PLATE 3

PLATE 4

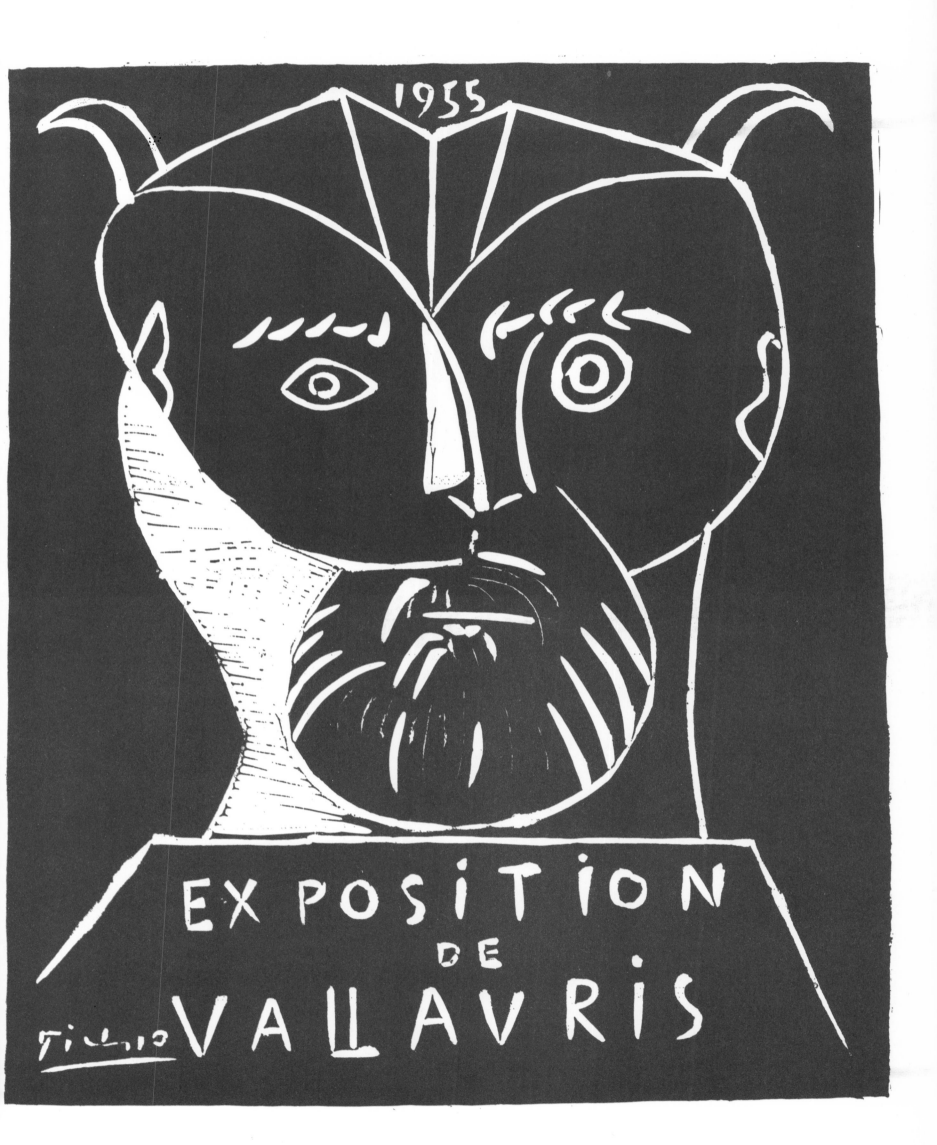

PLATE 5

LITHOGRAPHIES

de

PABLO PICASSO

pour

LE CHANT DES MORTS

de

PIERRE REVERDY

TÉRIADE ÉDITEUR

EXPOSITION

chez

LOUIS CARRÉ

10, Avenue de Messine, Paris-8ᵉ

DU 17 AU 31 DÉCEMBRE 1948

PLATE 6

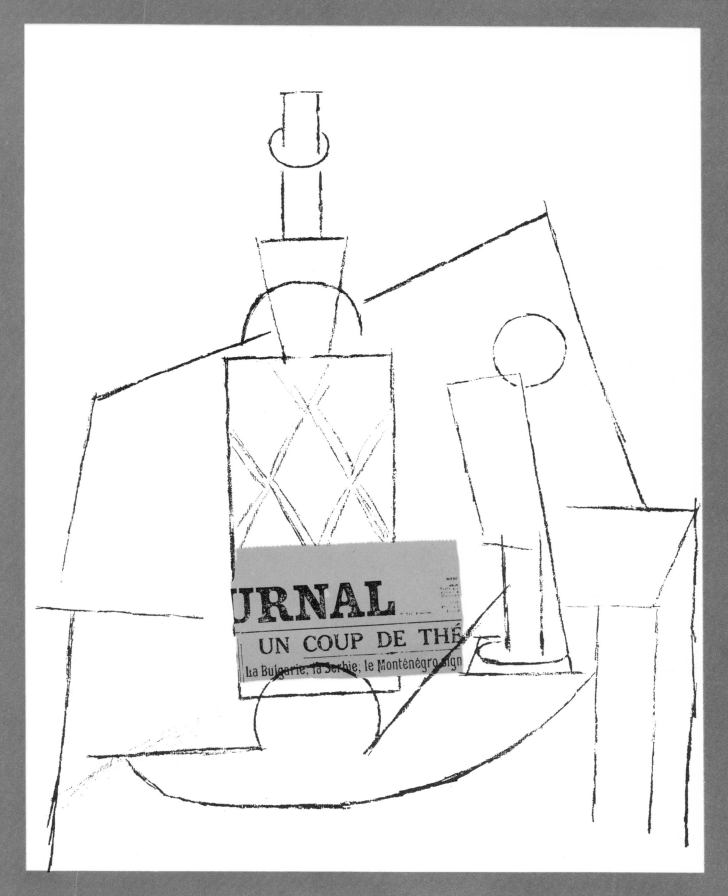

PICASSO

PAPIERS COLLÉS - DESSINS

AU PONT DES ARTS - GALERIE LUCIE WEILL

6 RUE BONAPARTE - ODE 71-95

26 JANVIER - 16 FÉVRIER 1956

PLATE 7

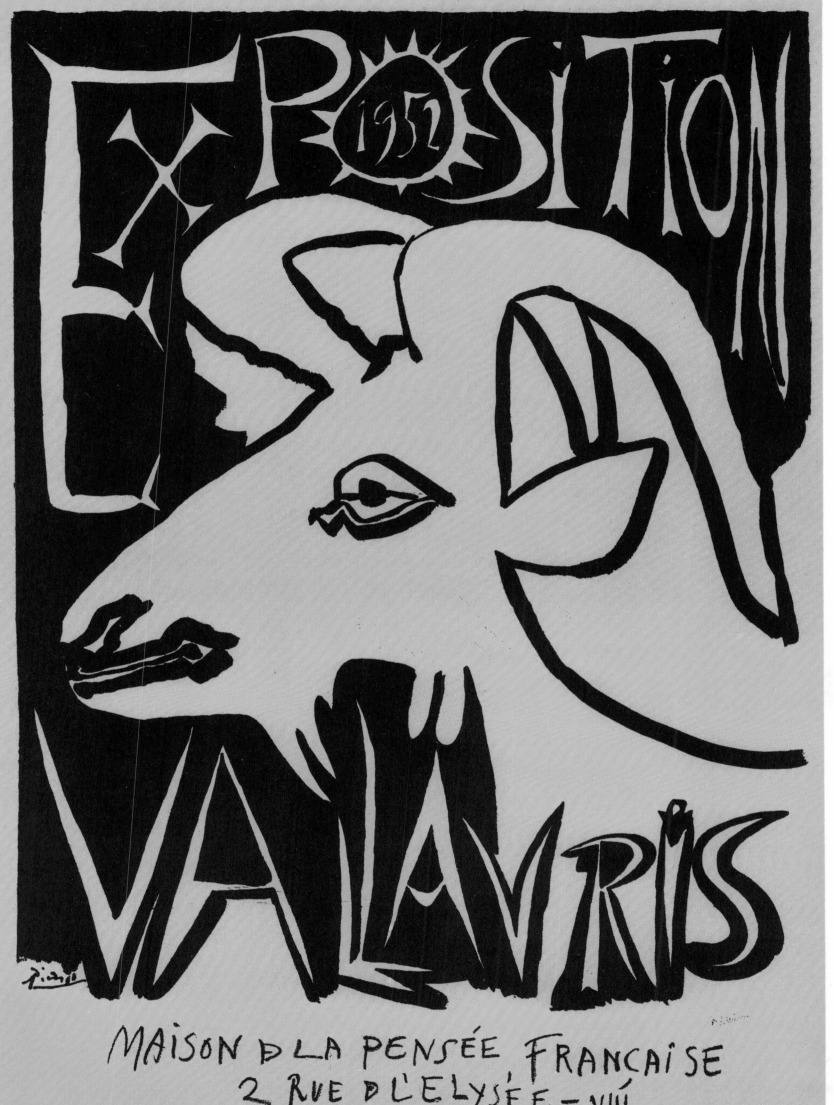

PLATE 8

VALLAURIS
EXPOSITION 1954

PLATE 9

Picasso
R.1.51.

JMP. DE LA VICTOIRE - NICE

PLATE 10

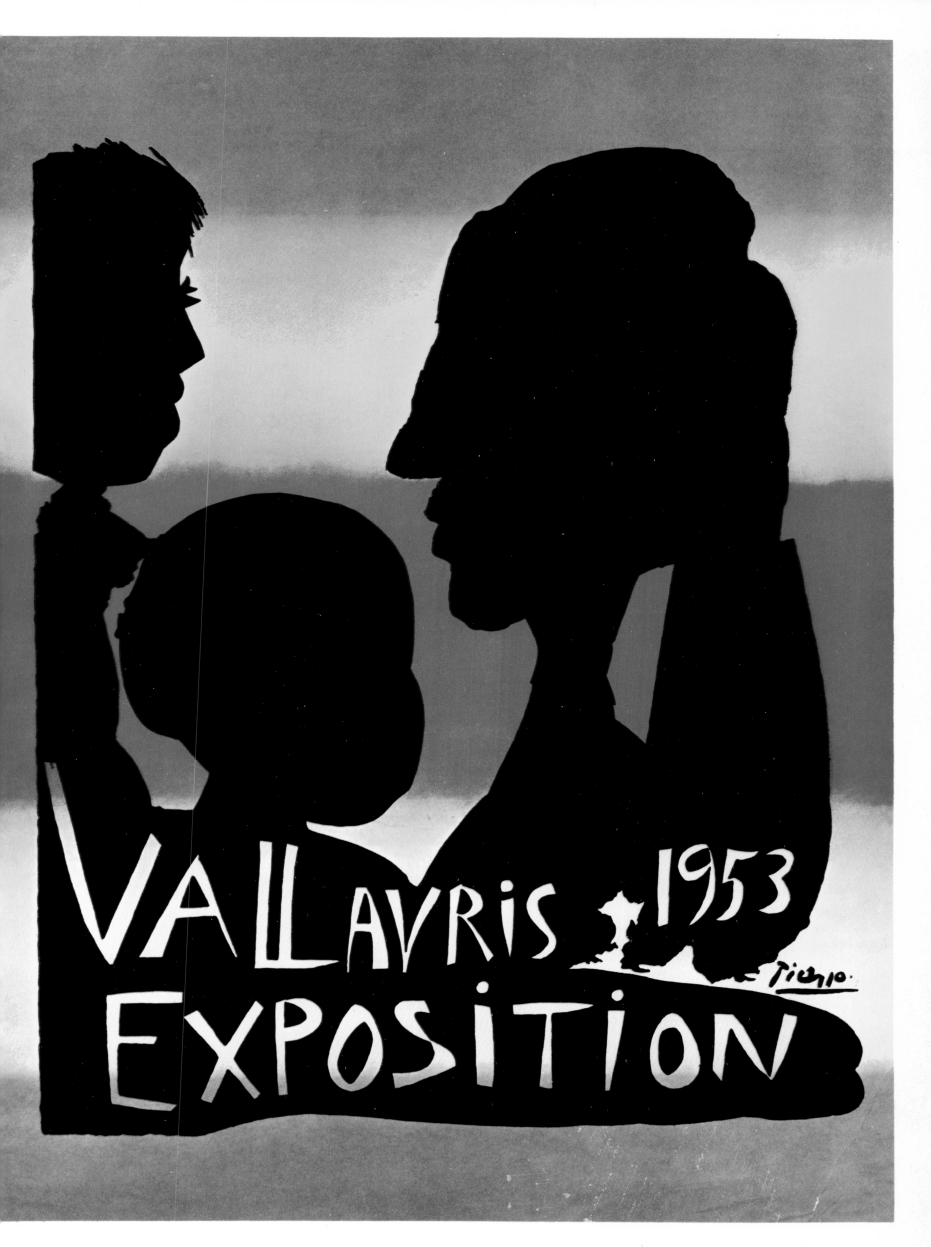

PLATE 11

ピカソ展

11月6日-25日

日本橋 髙島屋

主催 読売新聞社

PLATE 12

PLATE 13

GALERIE 65
CANNES

Picasso

14 AÔUT – 30 Septembre 1956

PLATE 14

PICASSO
PEINTURES
1955—1956
GALERIE LOUISE LEIRIS
47 Rue de Monceau — PARIS — VIII
MARS — AVRIL 1957.

PLATE 15

PLATE 16

CONGRÈS MONDIAL
DES PARTISANS
DE LA PAIX

SALLE PLEYEL
20·21·22 ET 23 AVRIL 1949
PARIS

MOURLOT_ IMP. PARIS

PLATE 17

Hommage des
artistes Espagnols
au poète Antonio
Machado

Exposition

peinture - Sculpture
du 4 au 24 Février 1955

Maison de la Pensée Française
2 Rue de l'Elysée
PARIS VIII

Picasso
le 3.1.55.

PLATE 18

PLATE 19

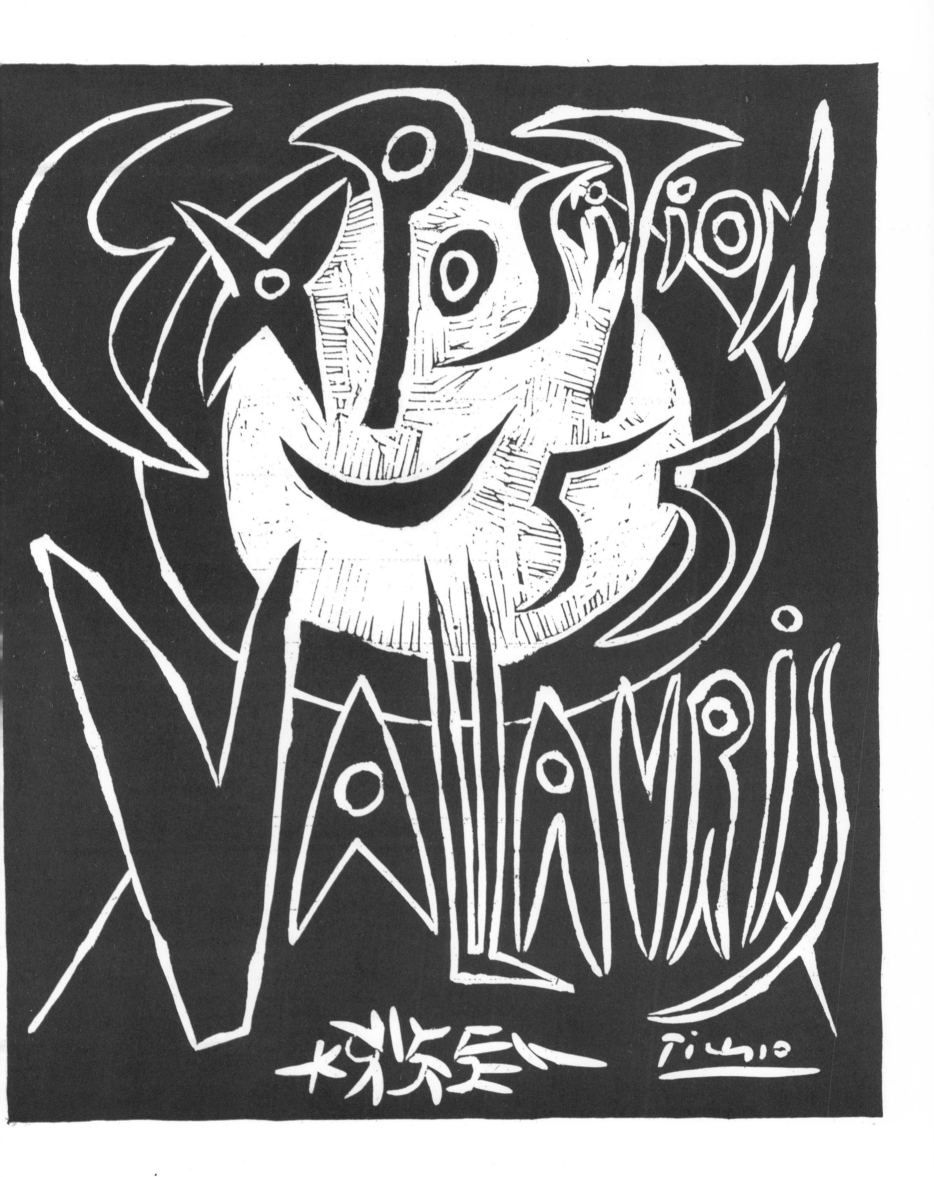

PLATE 20

PLATE 21

PLATE 22

PLATE 23

POUR PARAITRE LE 15 OCTOBRE 1954

SUITE

DE 180

DESSINS

DE

PICASSO

28 NOVEMBRE 1953
AU 3 FÉVRIER 1954

VERVE 29-30

PLATE 24